BOARD BASICS

A Primer for Nonprofit Board Members

JERRY COVEY

ISBN: 1453720464
ISBN-13: 9781453720462
Library of Congress Control Number: 2010911021

Dedicated to Sandy,
who saw this book long before I did.

ACKNOWLEDGMENTS

Special thanks to friends who lent their professional expertise and time to make this book a reality. Duane Guiley, an
expert in nonprofit finance, patiently guided me through
the budget, audit, and risk management chapters. Norm
Wooten, a nonprofit board leader with decades of experience, shared valuable "board member" insights. Fred Lau,
a successful nonprofit leader in multiple economic sectors,
provided important attention to the details of governance.
Carl Rose, a longtime chief executive officer of a superb
state-level professional association that serves nonprofit
boards, has an understanding of board governance and
executive leadership that shows up all through this book.
Finally, thanks to the board members and clients who, over
the years, taught me through example what board members must know and do to succeed. Without all of you, this
book would never have been completed.

LIST OF TABLES

TABLE OF CONTENTS

INTRODUCTION

You joined your board to make a difference—whether it was to improve services, make better use of resources, change your organization's direction, or protect important commitments. You cared enough to step forward, and you want your board service to produce results that are important to you and those you represent.

If you're a new board member, *Board Basics* will bring you up to speed quickly; will help you understand your role, responsibilities, limits, and level of authority; and will provide information about the tools and processes that will help you make sound decisions.

If you're a seasoned veteran, reading *Board Basics* will provide the opportunity to revisit core governance principles and compare them with your board's current practices. It will also invite reflection on your own growth and development as a board member and spur you to give newcomers to your board a leg up on avoiding beginners' mistakes that would set back their growth and development.

Additionally, as you'll learn in the following chapters, *Board Basics* will help you successfully steer your way through the politics that comes with governance—with your integrity intact.

ONE FINAL POINT before you begin *Board Basics:* As a board member, your power and authority are always limited—and your opportunities to create something better are always limitless.

CHAPTER 1
NEW BOARD MEMBER ORIENTATION

There's no substitute for a strong start to your board service. Quickly becoming informed prepares you to participate effectively in resolving governance issues and gives you confidence to contribute to the success of your organization.

Seasoned board members have definite opinions about the value of their orientations and, if asked, are usually quick to state them. Board members who received a well-crafted and well-delivered orientation say it allowed them to hit the deck running, while those whose orientation was poorly organized or nonexistent recall feelings of frustration, confusion, embarrassment over avoidable mistakes, and, most of all, anger and disappointment that no one helped them.

As a high-performing CEO* put it, "You must understand the framework of the organization to succeed as a board member." This chapter provides that framework.

---

* In this book, I use the terms *CEO* and *chief executive officer* to refer collectively to the administrator in charge of organizational leadership and administration. Other frequently used terms are *executive director, director,* and *chief administrative officer.*

TWO-PART ORIENTATION

Success in any endeavor depends in part on receiving the training and information needed at the appropriate time. With that in mind, a practical way of delivering your orientation is to divide it into two parts.

Part one is the initial orientation. This orientation is tailored to answer questions you have and to provide information that prepares you for your first board meeting and other board events that will occur in the near future.

Part two is the just-in-time orientation that delivers information about specific events as they arise on the board's calendar of activities.

Let's look closely at those two orientation processes to discover how they provide information and training at the appropriate times.

PART ONE: INITIAL ORIENTATION

You arrive with unique skills and experiences. Perhaps you're a veteran of other boards, ready to begin your service with minimal assistance, or you may be a first-time board member with no experience and limited understanding of your governance role. Either way, your orientation should be tailored to help you succeed.

A practical way of beginning the initial orientation is to obtain answers to questions you may have about your board service or the organization you're now charged with governing. Once that's been accomplished, the focus of that meeting should be on preparing you for your first board meeting by providing you with an overview of the organization, ensuring you have access to important information you'll need, and assigning you a contact and/ or mentor to answer further questions and guide you through unfamiliar territory.

FIRST MEETING

Let's begin with your board packet. A board packet contains the information you'll need to review and understand before the board president gavels the meeting to order. If a board packet is not offered for your review, ask to see one and have someone explain the details in it. You'll want to know how the agenda is organized, how information included in the packet is related to the agenda, how many days before the meeting you'll receive your board packet, how to get an item placed on the agenda, and whom to contact if you have questions about it. Stay with the board packet discussion until you're comfortable that you know what to expect at the meeting and how to prepare for it.

SYSTEMS AND STRUCTURE OVERVIEW

Following the board packet conversation, turn your attention to the big picture to gain an overview of the organization's systems and structure.

Organizations rely on systems that serve specific functions to ensure that important tasks are accomplished routinely and successfully. As a board member, you'll need a general understanding of those systems and how they're coordinated to produce desired results. Your organiza-tion's structure may be shown as an organizational chart that identifies major systems, illustrates who reports to whom in the organization, and designates the positions assigned to each system. The CEO drafts and modifies the organizational chart to keep it current with changes in structure. (Part two of your orientation will further detail the organizational systems and structure.)

GUIDE TO SUCCESS

The value of having a contact person to answer your initial questions about board service and the contents of your board packet has already been mentioned. Now, let's extend that idea to your first few months or longer of board service. If you're new to board governance, there's no substitute for access to someone who has experience in the organization and with whom you can connect as needed. If this option is not offered to you, ask for it.

DOCUMENTS

To govern successfully, you'll need access to docu-ments containing information about your organization. Fortunately, much of that information is now available in digital format, which will certainly lighten your load. Following is a list of documents to which board members typically have ready access. Use the list as a starting point to confirm what information you'll need, and, if necessary, ask someone to demonstrate how to obtain it.

Documents that board members typically have access to include:

- Board committee assignments
- Board goals
- Board meeting and events schedules
- Bylaws/policies
- CEO contract
- Compensation/benefits information
- Critical-issues list
- Latest financial audit report
- Operating budget
- Organizational chart
- Organizational performance data
- Organizational plans
- Risk management plan if applicable

PART TWO: JUST-IN-TIME ORIENTATION

Certain major board activities—such as budget development, financial audit, and board and CEO evaluations—occur on annual cycles, while others—such as approval of capital projects, bond issues, and employee negotiations—occur on an as-needed basis.

Delivering a just-in-time orientation for each of the following topics ensures that you'll have the information you need fresh in your mind—when you need it.

TYPICAL ANNUAL OR CYCLICAL ORIENTATION TOPICS

- Board goals
- Board policy review
- Board self-evaluation
- Budget development
- Financial audit
- New board member orientation
- Political action strategies
- Program review/evaluation

- CEO evaluation

- Employee contract negotiations

- Review/renewal of board memberships

- Strategic plan update

AS-NEEDED ORIENTATION TOPICS

- Architectural plans
- Bonding/insurance review/renewal
- Capital projects/bond issues

- Construction schedules
- Project development calendar
- Risk management information

QUESTIONING NEW BOARD MEMBER ORIENTATION

1. When did your board last review its new member orientation process?
2. What specific recommendations, if any, were made to improve the process?
3. Do your state and/or national professional associations provide guidance for orientation of new board members?
4. Does your board offer or provide mentoring for new members by senior members during new members' first year of service?
5. What recommendations would you make for improving new board member orientation?

ONE FINAL POINT

The quality of orientation you receive is indicative of the value your organization places on helping newcomers get off to a strong start.

CHAPTER 2
COMMUNICATION

Place communication at the forefront of board member skills, because nothing outweighs the abilities to listen, understand, successfully share ideas, and skillfully influence communication in an increasingly connected world.

WELCOME TO THE BOARD

For new board members, the first communication lesson is that their words and writing take on whole new meanings when their messages affect the hopes, dreams, and livelihoods of others.

Seasoned board members have said that the volume and intensity of communications they encountered when they joined their boards initially caught them off guard. Some were confronted with demands, some had to field unsolicited opinions, and some faced exaggerated expectations they had not anticipated and were unprepared to address.

One woman said that after her appointment to a hospital board and prior to her first board meeting, she was invited by a longtime friend and hospital employee to visit her at work for coffee. Eager to visit, the new appointee accepted but became quite startled to find that instead of the anticipated personal visit she expected, she found herself in a room full of employees who had a long list of gripes and demands.

New board members may envision successful conversations that produce positive feelings and outcomes. While such conversations are enjoyable and always appreciated, veteran board members know that communicating successfully often includes telling people things they don't want to hear or tackling issues that are emotionally charged or philosophically divisive.

COMMUNICATIONS BASICS

Although communicating with others has its challenges, there are strategies you can use to help mitigate many communication difficulties.

RESPECT

First and foremost, treat every person with respect. Respect is the platform of reason; it honors people, demonstrates genuine consideration and thoughtfulness, and helps focus conversation on the issues at hand. People who are treated with respect usually return it. Additionally, they're often more rational and less likely to become angry or defensive if their ideas are not embraced.

LISTENING

Genuine undivided attention expressed by appropriate eye contact and body language is a powerful communication tool. People are attracted to listeners whose actions demonstrate they care about the conversation. Whether in agreement or not with the speaker, attentive listeners take conversations seriously and show regard for others through their words and actions. They ask questions to clarify the accuracy of their understanding, and they interrupt politely if it is necessary to do so. To confirm that their understanding is accurate, they take the initiative to restate what they think they heard another say. By staying connected in a conversation, good listeners assure the speaker that he or she has been respected, heard, and understood.

STYLE AND CONTEXT

Versatility and flexibility are trademarks of skilled communicators. Skillful communicators are tied to principles first and positions second. They are open to learning and looking for new ways to address issues that satisfy their own positions and interests as well as the positions and interests of parties that see things differently.

Skilled communicators know from experience that they will encounter individuals and groups with communication styles and behaviors that may be unfamiliar or challenging.

Take the issue of context as an example. Context is often referred to as perspective or attitude. An individual or a group's context significantly affects the way it approaches conversations and deals with challenging issues. A glass-half-full person operating from a position of confidence and optimism will participate differently in a challenging conversation from a glass-half-empty person who's focused on what's wrong or what will likely go wrong.

People select their communication styles and behaviors for each interaction based on their attitudes, perceptions, skills, and previous experiences. Understanding the context others bring to a conversation increases the opportunity to interact successfully with them.

The following table shows four common types of communicating styles. Beneath each style are descriptions of some of the characteristics or behaviors pertinent to that style.

Table I: Communication Styles

PASSIVE	Passive AGGRESSIVE	Active AGGRESSIVE	ASSERTIVE
• Has difficulty making decisions • Is nervous and or shy • Has difficulty saying no • Sends mixed messages • Is tearful or cries	• Talks behind a person's back • Tries to make other person feel guilty • Rolls eyes, sighs, mumbles • Refuses to respond to other person • Questions intentions of others	• Violates the rights of others • Is sarcastic and confrontational • Blames and accuses others, name calls, swears • Acts disrespectfully • Makes threats, gets physical	• Actively engages in meeting the needs of others • Expresses both positive and negative opinions and feelings • Is sensitive to the feelings and rights of others • Objects to behaviors that infringe on the rights of others • Is brief and to the point • Treats others with respect

Additional factors that may affect communication style include a person's emotional state, personal characteristics, background culture, and personal limitations.

RUMORS

As the old story goes, a rumor can go all the way around the world before the truth can get off to a good start. Dealing with rumors can be a challenge! One successful approach to dealing with rumors is to investigate them as quickly as possible and then gather factual information and communicate it to the appropriate people promptly in order to dispel incorrect information. Although doing that takes time and resources, it also sets the record straight and demonstrates that your organization is concerned about accuracy and is responsive to issues raised by others.

BOARD ISSUES AND MEDIA

In our increasingly connected world, the items before your board and the actions of your board can become known by almost anyone who has even a casual interest. Technology-driven media now provide opportunities for individuals as well as local, state, national, and international interest groups to quickly zero in on what your board is doing. In addition, those individuals and groups can use resources at their own disposal to influence the direction of your organization and the actions of your board.

Media communication is an important issue for every organization; it is an ongoing subject of books and seminars; and it may be a topic of interest for your board's professional development. Short of training in ways to communicate successfully with the media, a few basics will serve you well. First, determine whether your board has a policy or protocol for communicating with the media. Second, if media communication is among your responsibilities, take the initiative to establish and maintain a positive relationship with media officials. Third, respond to media quickly and accurately. Fourth, do not speak on issues about which you are not well informed. If you don't know the answer, say so and add that you will obtain the information and get back to them. Then do just that. Fifth, know ahead of time when to redirect their questions to others.

Upgrading your communication skills is a must to succeed in a media-rich and constantly changing global environment that comprises well-connected interest groups, rapidly shifting economies, and technology that in an instant can connect millions of people worldwide.

The importance of successfully engaging in communications with individuals and groups with which you directly or indirectly engage poses significant challenges to governing boards and their members.

QUESTIONING COMMUNICATION

1. Does the board have bylaws or policies regarding communication by board members to individuals or groups?
2. Does the organization provide communication training for board members?
3. Does the board assign spokespersons to respond to the media on specific issues?
4. Does the board critique itself on communications as part of its annual evaluation?
5. Does the organization have an effective process for dealing with rumors and misinformation?

ONE FINAL POINT

No matter what anyone tells you, when you're a board member there's no such thing as an off-the-record comment.

CHAPTER 3
BUDGET

Budgets make or break organizations. At best, they underwrite the mission, support priorities, and affect desired outcomes. At worst, they squander opportunities, destroy trust, and fail to meet legal obligations.

Budgets frequently evoke strong feelings because so much depends on them. Every salary, service, trip, activity, product, facility, and meeting is affected by a budget, and board members sometimes get an earful from administrators, constituents, and interest groups on how to develop, modify, or vote on them.

Working with budgets affects board members differently. For some, budgets are pleasurable and easy to work with and understanding them comes naturally. At the other extreme are board members who find themselves confused and frustrated by terminology, formats, and formulas they do not understand.

Regardless of your personal comfort level with budgets, getting a handle on the ones that require your vote and oversight is a front-burner issue. Knowing the what and the why of budgets increases your confidence and supports informed decision making. Fortunately, getting up to speed on budgets is not as difficult as it may seem. With the right help, you can quickly learn budget basics and be ready to vote with understanding and confidence.

BUDGET BASICS

A budget is a financial plan intended to ensure money is available to purchase goods and services that support your organization's activities.

Not-for-profit organizational budgets typically focus on expenses and are developed on an annual basis—usually a fiscal year or calendar year. Budgets are also developed on a project basis that could be shorter or longer than a year.

The board is the final authority on all budgets and is legally responsible for developing, approving, monitoring, and modifying them. Your board policies explain both the board's and the CEO's budget responsibilities and authority. As a board member, you will be privy to and responsible for maintaining confidential budget information.

HOW BUDGETS ARE BUILT

In theory, budgets are built on organizational goals, plans, and purposes. In reality, they're built on current obligations, previous budgets, and annual revenue projections. Organizations typically look to both the past and the present to build budgets for the future. While there are good reasons for that practice, it lends itself to budgeting for the status quo versus the future.

On one hand, looking at previous and current budgets provides an accurate view of historical expenditure patterns, recognizes obligations and commitments, and supports the continuation of successful programs and activities. On the other hand, your organization's environment is constantly changing. New challenges and opportunities require reallocation of limited resources. A well-built budget balances the best programs and services of the present with the opportunities and challenges of the future.

ASSUMPTIONS, GOALS, AND PLANS

The appropriate first step in building a budget is for the board to develop budget assumptions for staff members who will work up a draft budget. Budget assumptions are statements that communicate the board's intentions and priorities for the coming year. For example, if the board decides to spend down a fund balance, change the staffing formula, or commit to a new program or service, those assumptions should be communicated to staff prior to development of the draft budget.

DEVELOPMENT PROCESS

The actual process and timelines for budget development are often set forth in the board policy and may include direct board involvement, committee work, constituent input, and public hearings. Once the development process is completed, the final draft of the budget is presented to the board for its review and approval prior to enactment. Note, however, that during the development process, steps taken by the board to reallocate resources are often accompanied by interest group resistance, which can be disruptive. While it might be easier for the sake of peace to live with commitments that add little or nothing to the quality of programs or services, doing so limits future opportunities for the organization you govern.

At its completion, the draft budget is presented to the board for its final review and, if necessary, revision prior to adoption.

FORMAT

The way budget information gets arranged is known as the budget format. Budget formats are typically developed to meet specific legal, accounting, or funding-agency requirements and, as a result, may not be user friendly. Fortunately, many CEOs and finance officers are adept at formatting budget information in ways that help board members successfully manage budgets for which they are responsible. No matter what format is used, you must understand the budget and be able to explain it. If you can't, ask for help, and stay with the discussion until you gain the necessary understanding.

WORKING WITH YOUR BUDGET
BUDGET OVERSIGHT AND BUDGET MANAGEMENT

Budget oversight is solely the responsibility of the board. It begins with the aforementioned development of budget assumptions and board approval and continues with ongoing periodic reviews of budget management and organizational performance. It is important to clarify that while boards oversee budgets, they do not manage them. A board that has questions about the budget should direct them to the CEO.

Budget development and management are executive responsibilities delegated by the board to the CEO. The CEO and the CEO's staff have specific training and expertise in budget development and management. They also have firsthand knowledge of the day-to-day operating environment. That knowledge provides them with important insights and judgment. Specific budget management authority and responsibilities are often written into board policies, administrative job descriptions, and employment contracts. An example would be authority granted by a board to the CEO for expenditures up to preset limits without board involvement.

BUDGET VARIANCE OR EXCEPTION

Depending on the organization, a budget can be developed and approved a month or more before it gets implemented and, as a result, may not reflect increases in operating costs or changes in plans that may have occurred in the interim.

Actual or projected revenue or expenditures that exceed the budgeted amount by a predetermined limit are known as budget variances or exceptions and are correctable only by a board action known as a budget amendment or adjustment. It's the CEO's responsibility to alert the board about variances and to recommend either transferring funds within the budget to cover the additional costs or moving funds to reserves.

BUDGET DISCIPLINE

Governing boards and CEOs must exercise unswerving self-discipline regarding the budget.

A board that crosses the line from budget oversight to budget management usurps the authority and responsibility of the CEO. Such actions short-circuit the balance of power and deny the board access to the professional skill and judgment of its hired executive. A board that assumes management prerogatives must also assume responsibility for the results. Likewise, a CEO must refrain from leading the board to take actions that short-circuit the board's ability to be the arbiter and protector of stakeholder interests.

The board is the ultimate authority regarding financial commitments and is liable for actions taken on behalf of the organization. It bears repeating that the board's budget role consists of policy and oversight; the CEO's role consists of administration of day-to-day operations.

If your board has concerns about the quality of financial management being provided by the CEO, it should not involve itself directly in managing the organization's finances. It should instead call for an independent audit to verify that the financial representations of management and the integrity of the financial management system are accurate and sound.

BUDGET TERMINOLOGY

account	a classification of revenue or expense
appropriate	to accept, allocate, and plan a specific use for revenue
asset	property that has a specific value and is owned by the organization
audit	an official examination and verification of financial activity by an internal or external body
budget	an estimate of expected income and expenses for a given period of time
budget assumption	statements of the board's intent for the upcoming year expressed in terms of budget priorities
budget calendar	statement that prescribes a time frame for developing the budget

budget exception or variance

an expense or revenue that exceeds the amount approved for an expense by a predetermined limit and requires board action to address

budget oversight

review of budget activities carried out by the board to ensure consistency with goals and plans as well as compliance with laws, regulations, and policies

calendar year

a continuous, twelve-month year beginning January 1 and ending December 31

chart of accounts

a standardized code representing the rules, policies, and regulations that are applied for developing and reporting budget information

encumbrance

funding set aside to cover an expense that has not been paid for

fiscal year

a continuous, twelve-month year beginning and ending on predetermined dates

liability

a financial obligation

QUESTIONING BUDGET

1. How does your board determine the amount of detail desired in the budget information provided by the CEO? Is it satisfied with the current level of detail?
2. How much does it cost your organization to operate per day? Per week? Per month?
3. What happens to money left in the operating budget at the end of the year?
4. How much income does your organization receive, and what is its source?
5. How much, if any, of your organization's income is guaranteed?

ONE FINAL POINT

The operational principle of "trust but verify" serves board members well when it comes to budget oversight. Boards that don't stay on top of their budgets often find themselves confronted with unanticipated complications and will have to deal with issues after the fact.

Chapter 4
Audit

An audit is an independent examination of official records that validates those records' accuracy by measuring samples of the records against legal requirements, audit standards, and policies established by the board. Audits can be conducted at any time but may be required annually by federal and state mandates, funding agencies, and board policies or decisions.

People often think of finances when they hear the word "audit," but boards also use audits to measure compliance with and performance against established rules and/or program standards. Public-sector and not-for-profit organizations are often required to conduct annual revenue and expenditure audits that provide historical information about how funds were used.

An audit is not an assurance that all records are in order. Instead, it provides a snapshot by reviewing a sampling of various records to determine their consistency and accuracy as they relate to applicable policies.

CONFLICT OF INTEREST

Conflict-of-interest issues may arise when boards or CEOs hire auditors who in turn report to them. The concern in such instances is that the auditors may be "beholden" to their employer and may tend to sanitize the audit results by overlooking or minimizing problems that get discovered. To address that concern, some states require—and some boards elect—the appointment of independent finance and/or audit committees to hire the auditor and receive the audit report.

Congress passed the Sarbanes-Oxley Act in 2002 to address accounting scandals by publicly traded for-profit corporations, and it has resulted in state and local laws and regulations that involve financial management of nonprofit organizations. Ask whether your organization takes voluntary or required actions to address provisions of the Sarbanes-Oxley Act for public entities as the act applies to nonprofit organizations.

THE BOARD'S ROLE IN THE AUDIT

Boards hire auditors the same way they hire other professional service providers. Once hired, an auditor works closely with the CEO and the CEO's staff to conduct the audit; however, the auditor's first responsibility is always to the board. Once the audit is completed, it is presented to the board.

As a board member, you may not actually meet face to face with the auditor until the audit is completed and presented to the board. At that time, you can ask questions of the auditor regarding anything in the audit report. If you or other members of the board have audit questions before or during the audit, you should direct them to your CEO.

As part of its fiduciary responsibility, the board may choose to meet in executive session with the auditor—independent of staff members—to ask questions about the audit.

PREPARING FOR THE AUDIT

Following are some terms and definitions you will encounter when you read or listen to audit presentations.

audit controls	safeguards put in place to ensure that internal controls are sufficient to protect an organization's assets
capital asset	material wealth in the form of money or property to which a specific value has been assigned
compliance	test of transactions against a third-party standard

contingency
a potential future event that might arise and must be planned for

financial statement
presentation of financial data that shows an organization's financial position at a specific point in time

fund balance
money remaining in an account after the purpose for which it was meant has been satisfied

inventory
list of current assets, including property and supplies on hand

liability
legal responsibility for existing or potential costs or damages

management letter
narrative letter from the auditor that states the results of the audit

opinion letter
statement of the auditor's findings: an *unqualified opinion* means no problems were found in the audit; a *qualified letter* indicates problems, explains them, and identifies a remedy

performance	measurement against a prede-termined standard
representation letter	letter from the CEO to the auditor saying all information furnished to the auditor is accurate

QUESTIONING AUDIT

1. When was the last time your board changed the auditor(s)?
2. Does your organization have significant liabilities, and if so, what are they?
3. What safeguards are in place to protect the treasury?
4. Are there internal issues about which the board should know?
5. Is there anything in the management letter about which the board should be concerned?

ONE FINAL POINT

Many boards select different auditing firms after four or five years to ensure a fresh review and a new look at the integrity of their financial records management.

CHAPTER 5
RISK MANAGEMENT

Risk is a level of uncertainty organizations encounter as a result of their existence, activities, and assets. Risk management is a planned approach to manage those uncertainties in ways that minimize the likelihood of threats and losses.

At first glance, many board members consider risk management an insurance issue; in reality, risk management is much more. Although the purchase of insurance is an important part of a risk management plan, your first order of business is to understand your organization's risk environment and know your options to address it.

UNDERSTANDING YOUR RISK ENVIRONMENT

Begin by asking what risks your organization is exposed to, how significant they are, and what strategies are used to address them. You'll need the advice of an insurance professional to answer those questions.

Typically, an insurance broker provides this service when it's time to consider renewal of the organization's insurance policies. While the board is meeting with the broker to review risk management issues, keep in mind

that although the broker has expertise in risk management and provides you with the best advice, the broker
is not neutral when it comes to the policies and amounts
of coverage to sell.

RISK MANAGEMENT OPTIONS

The board has three options available to address risks.

1. Transfer the risks to someone else. This is known
   as the golden rule of risk.
2. Eliminate the risks.
3. Retain the risks.

Let's look more closely at each option.

OPTION ONE: THE GOLDEN RULE OF RISK MANAGEMENT

The golden rule of risk management is to transfer risk to
someone else. Ah, if only we could afford to purchase all
the insurance we wanted! Transfer of risk is accomplished
either by purchasing insurance to cover liabilities or by
requiring those who do business with your organization
to carry enough insurance to cover the cost of claims likely
to arise from the course of their work.

OPTION TWO: ELIMINATE THE RISK

Discontinuing or avoiding some activities may be prefer-
able to assuming the risk they produce. For example, since

the 1980s, organizations have been actively removing asbestos from their buildings because of the health risk asbestos poses. More recently, many organizations have banned smoking in buildings for the same reason.

A third-party risk management review may reveal risks that have become transparent to your organization because of the organization's longtime exposure to them. Plus, you may discover significant risk factors linked to programs or activities that are of questionable value to the organization. In other words, the risk may outweigh the benefits of certain programs or activities.

OPTION THREE: RETAIN THE RISK

It's not possible to transfer or eliminate all risks. Some level of risk is inherent, a reality of existence. Deciding which types and what amounts of risk to retain is a judgment call that is appropriately reserved for your governing board and should be made based on the best risk management information available.

CONSIDER A PERIODIC RISK MANAGEMENT REVIEW

Risk management duties do not typically rate high on the list of board member responsibilities; however, understanding risk and actively managing it is far superior to suffering catastrophic consequences.

One of the attractive options for boards is to hire an independent risk management consultant to review the board's risk management plan, report on the plan's strengths and weaknesses, and, if necessary, make recommendations to improve the plan. A neutral third-party risk management review combined with your organization's insurance broker's and CEO's reviews will provide additional insight into your organization's risk environment and will confirm whether current risk management practices meet industry standards.

Revisit Your Risk Management Plan

Satisfy yourself that the board is making the best choices to transfer, eliminate, or retain the risks it faces. Keep in mind that while it is common to act based on expert advice, it is better to act based on a thorough examination of your organization's plan and your own conviction that the board's choice of risk management strategies provides the most prudent and most comprehensive protection for the organization.

Questioning Risk Management

1. When was the last time the board conducted a formal risk management review?
2. If the board has conducted reviews in the past, has the board included an independent third-party risk management expert?

3. How does your risk management plan compare with the plans of organizations of similar size and purpose?
4. Do you have an insurance policy to cover any errors or omissions made by the governing board?
5. Have you put your risk management package out to competitive bid in recent years?

ONE FINAL POINT

Find out exactly what protections are in place to protect individual board members from liability for their governance decisions.

Chapter 6
Shared Leadership

The structure of nonprofit organizations intentionally divides authority and responsibility for leadership between the governing board and the CEO. Details about the specific authority and responsibilities of the board and of the CEO are set forth in the organization's policies, the organization's bylaws, and the employment contract of the CEO. This practical and balanced power-sharing arrangement creates specific authority and responsibility for the board and for the CEO.

DEFINED ROLES

As a general rule, the board guides the activities of the organization indirectly through policy and holds it accountable by monitoring results and, if necessary, by taking corrective action.

Specifically, the board fulfills its function primarily in the following ways: It determines the organization's purpose, or mission, and its direction, or vision. It creates policy to ensure that the organization's business is conducted legally and ethically. The board allocates resources to support organizational activities, and it monitors the results of those activities. It serves as the arbiter and protector of all stakeholder interests. As such, the board has the authority and responsibility to exercise its judgment and intervene when appropriate to ensure that actions taken on behalf of the organization comply with requirements and are in the best interest of the organization.

The CEO, typically the only employee who reports directly to the board, has specific authority and responsibility delegated by the board to lead and manage the organization's resources and activities. Whereas the board's role is to guide the organization indirectly, the CEO is responsible for hands-on leadership, which includes managing all resources, establishing and implementing processes to conduct organizational activities, monitoring performance, ensuring that all requirements are met, building organizational capacity, and improving performance. Additionally, the CEO is accountable to the board for all results.

The tables on pages 42-43 illustrate and explain the division of authority and responsibility for the board/ CEO relationship.

LEADERSHIP DISCIPLINE

Dividing leadership authority and responsibility between the board and the CEO makes for a balanced and effective structure. That said, conducting the organization's business within those constraints can be, at times, challenging for both board members and the CEO.

On one hand, if board members get involved in executive decisions, it diffuses the CEO's authority and leads to employees, individuals, and interest groups playing board members and administrators against each other. On the other hand, if the board is too far removed from day-to-day activities, it becomes overly dependent on the CEO and may not be getting the real stories about issues or activities that affect the organization. Likewise, when a CEO crosses the line and dictates policy to the board, that CEO usurps the board's authority and responsibility to balance the public's interests and weakens the link between the board and its constituents.

When board members or CEOs cross the invisible line between their areas of responsibility and authority and those of their counterparts, they typically rationalize the appropriateness of their actions as most expedient to accomplish a specific purpose, and, of course, it's supposedly only for this one special situation. However, regardless of their rationalization or the outcome of their actions, they eventually pay a price for their actions.

Table 2

LEADERSHIP ROLES AND RESPONSIBILITIES
SHARED LEADERSHIP
DEFINED ROLES

Governing Board	*Chief Executive Officer (CEO)*
Arbiter/Protector of Stakeholder Interests	*Leadership Expert*
Governance Expertise	*Operational Expert*
Final Authority on All Matters NOT Delegated	*Final Authority on SPECIFICALLY Delegated Matters*
What	*How*
Policy	*Procedure*
Strategy Development	*Strategy Deployment*
Results	*Evaluation*

Table 3

LEADERSHIP ROLES AND RESPONSIBILITIES DEFINITIONS

GOVERNING BOARD	CEO
The final authority and responsibility for all actions of the organization rest here. The board can delegate its authority but not its responsibility.	The CEO is typically the board's only direct report.
Arbiter/Protector of Stakeholder Interests Through policy development, the board creates a structure to fairly and effectively conduct the organization's business and respond to stakeholder interests.	**Leadership Expert** The CEO is responsible for organizational leadership and workforce development.
Governance Expertise The board is responsible for ensuring that members have the skills and experience to govern successfully in a constantly changing environment.	**Operational Expert** The CEO is responsible for the design, implementation, and management of all organizational systems and processes.
Final Authority on All Matters _NOT_ Delegated As part of its shared leadership structure, the board retains authority to govern all undelegated operations of the organization.*	**Final Authority on _SPECIFICALLY_ Delegated Matters** Board policies and the CEO's employment contract specifically identify the CEO's authority and responsibility.
What The board guides the organization by keeping the focus on the organization's mission and vision.	**How** The CEO is responsible for translating the mission and vision of the board into actions that produce desired results.
Policy The board creates policies for the organization that direct and guide the organization's activities. The policies are legally enforceable.	**Procedure** The CEO develops written guidance for employees on how to implement the board's policies fairly and consistently.
Strategy Development Strategic thinking is a primary function of governance. Strategy drives policy, budget, and programs.	**Strategy Deployment** The CEO organizes and deploys resources to achieve organizational strategies set by the board.
Results Among its most critical tasks are monitoring organizational results and making adjustments to stay on course.	**Evaluation** The CEO is responsible for ensuring that timely and accurate evaluations are conducted on all organizational functions and that the results are reported to the board.

*Depending on the legal structure of the organization, the board's authority may be limited by the organization's constitution.

PLAY BY THE RULES, BECAUSE SOMEONE IS ALWAYS WATCHING

Whether disciplined or undisciplined, the actions and results leadership teams produce do not go unnoticed.

Those who work for or observe organizations are quick to see when leaders' actions do not align with written authority and responsibility. Inconsistent leadership behavior sends shock waves through organizations, resulting in confusion and uncertainty among employees and other stakeholders. Such leadership inconsistency invites mischief from both inside and outside the organization by those seeking to advance their own interests at the expense of the organization.

LONG-TERM VERSUS SHORT-TERM THINKING

The leadership challenges inherent in planning for the future and in deploying resources in an ever-changing environment require constant reevaluation and, when necessary, adjustments to stay true to an organization's mission and vision.

It is here that leadership is put to the true test, and here that high-performing organizations gain distance on their counterparts. Decisions regarding resource alignment, resource deployment, and process improvement are significantly affected by a short- versus long-term focus.

Interestingly, both high- and low-performing organizations operate based on bylaws and policies that are very similar; however, two things distinguish high-performing organizations from mid- and low-level performers. First and foremost is alignment of resources with mission and vision. High-performing organizations typically spend more effort working through varying assumptions and ideas to establish their priorities.

The second significant difference is discipline. Boards and CEOs of high-performing organizations make full use of their authority and fulfill their responsibilities as set forth in their organizations' policies and bylaws, but they stay out of each other's turf. In mid- and low-performing organizations, the division of authority and responsibility between the board and CEO gets less respect.

Governing boards and CEOs of high-performing organizations have much in common with teams that excel in any endeavor.

- Their purpose, known as **mission,** is well defined.
- They have a clear **vision** of where they want to go.
- Their core **values**—the behaviors expected of everyone in the organization—are nonnegotiable and evidenced in all their actions.
- They set specific **goals** and develop specific plans to accomplish them.
- They **measure** progress toward their goals consistently and accurately.
- They continually seek and find ways to **improve** their results.

Although the path to performance excellence varies from one high-performing organization to another, the architectures of each one's success are strikingly similar: purpose, vision, discipline, focus, commitment, measurable results, and a passion for improvement all show up consistently in their profiles.

QUESTIONING SHARED LEADERSHIP

1. How does the board and CEO monitor their own and each other's performance relative to staying within the limits of defined authority and responsibility?
2. What steps are taken if either the board or CEO oversteps their authority and/or responsibility?
3. Does the board treat organizational policies as laws they must abide by or as guidelines that are optional?
4. Would you say your board makes full use of its authority and responsibility in its governance role?
5. Would you say your CEO makes full use of CEO authority to lead your organization?

ONE FINAL POINT

Board control of an organization is established at the input level, not the outcome level. Once things are in motion, the board's job is to monitor results and hold others accountable.

Chapter 7
Board Meetings

Board Power

There's no such thing as an unimportant board meeting. At every meeting, your board makes decisions that affect organizational plans, goals, relationships, resources, programs, and people. It's only when the board is officially meeting that it has power to create bylaws and policies, set priorities, monitor performance, direct the CEO, and be the final authority on all matters not delegated.

While there is no single best way to conduct board meetings, there are conditions that, if met, promote meeting success.

Structure

Board meetings are conducted within a legal framework created by federal, state, and local governments and the policy framework of a board's own creation.

The best way for new board members to acquaint themselves with that framework is by consulting the bylaws section of the policy manual. Bylaws incorporate legal requirements with which boards must comply; they contain the board's own policies for conducting board meetings; and they speak to individual board member roles and responsibilities.

APPROPRIATE INFORMATION

Boards are dependent on the information they receive. Therefore, board packets must be well organized, effectively formatted, and user friendly. Board packets typically include the following items.

- **MEETING AGENDA**

  The meeting agenda should be an easy-to-read outline that identifies (1) items for presentation or discussion only and (2) action items that require a vote of the board. Last-minute additions to the agenda should be rare, because they defeat the board's efforts to be prepared for the meeting.

- **BOARD MEMORANDUM**

  This is a one-page synopsis for each action item. It provides important background information about the issue before the board, gives an explanation of the reason for the action proposed, suggests alternative methods for the board to address it, and includes the CEO's recommended action to the board. Additional supporting documents for each memorandum are placed immediately behind it in the board packet.

• WRITTEN PRESENTATIONS TO THE BOARD

These should be developed in formats that promote board understanding. Such items as government forms, technical specifications, and financial spreadsheets often contain unnecessary detail, present irrelevant information, and are in formats designed for other uses. When it's necessary to use technical data, the data should be reformatted if possible and thoroughly explained in a brief synoptic presentation prior to engaging the board in a question-and-answer session.

• ORAL PRESENTATIONS

Presentations to the board should be made in a synoptic format that states the issue up front, presents important background information, highlights important facts, identifies options, and provides rationales for a recommended course of action if appropriate. As a general rule, presentations to the board should be completed in three minutes or less to allow adequate time for board member questions and discussion. Complex presentations such as budgets, audits, and other lengthy issues may require special work sessions that allow time for adequate explanation and discussion.

MEETING PREPARATION AND PARTICIPATION

While board officers are responsible for conducting meetings in accordance with the organization's specific bylaws and policies, you and other board members have to perform the following responsibilities.

- **DO YOUR HOMEWORK**

  Read the board packet and arrive at the meeting prepared to participate in discussions and to examine every action item. Effective board members arrive with prepared comments and questions that help them gather information they need to fully understand the implications of proposed actions before they vote.

- **KNOW HOW A MEETING IS SUPPOSED TO WORK**

  Understand the roles of the board's officers and members and the role of the CEO in conducting a successful meeting. It is your duty to help the meeting stay on track and on time.

- **EXPECT THE BEST**

  Expect the best quality in written and oral presentations from the CEO and the CEO's subordinates and the best performance by all members of the board. Informed decisions depend on everyone's being up-to-date and informed on the issues and actively involved. Be quick to point out factors that negatively affect board-meeting quality.

- **ACT WITH INTEGRITY**

  Integrity is an all-or-nothing proposition; never sacrifice it for any reason. Decide your votes based on merits, not alliances. Acts of integrity uplift the entire organization.

- **PLAN THE TIMING**
  Allow adequate time to conduct business. A board meeting that has a comfortable rhythm, that sets a lively pace, and that produces informed debate and reasoned decisions is a thing of beauty. Such a meeting is also the result of thoughtful meeting design, careful materials preparation, use of effective meeting processes, and skilled communication. Efficient use of board-meeting time produces increased levels of effectiveness and board member satisfaction.

- **DISPLAY CIVILITY**
  Politeness and courtesy enhance all participants and support orderly and appropriate conduct of the board's business.

- **CULTIVATE EXECUTIVE SUPPORT**
  The greatest resource available to a board seeking to run successful and efficient meetings is the CEO. The CEO is expected to be the board's expert at setting the stage for effective board meetings. CEOs control the quality of material prepared for the board and establish parameters for staff members and consultants who interact with the board. They also advise and counsel the board on meeting processes and recommend board skill development related to improving the quality of board meetings.

- **EMPHASIZE TEAMWORK**

   Board members should never surprise their CEO at a meeting, and a CEO should never surprise the board.

QUESTIONING BOARD MEETINGS

1. Does your board receive professional development training in conducting quality meetings?
2. Does your board evaluate the quality of its meetings one or more times per year?
3. Are all members invited to participate during board meetings?
4. Are you aware of the board's bylaws and policies that have to do with meetings?
5. On a scale of 1 to 5, with 5 being the highest, how would you rate your organization's board meetings?

ONE FINAL POINT

No other individual or group has the board's continuous authority, power, or influence over your organization. Board decisions, made only when the board is in session, set the stage for organizational excellence, mediocrity, or failure.

Chapter 8
Professional Associations

Does your board belong to state and/or national professional organizations that provide services and products intended to further the agenda of the board and the skills of its members? If so, are you getting the bang for your buck?

At their best, professional organizations provide valuable services that support professional growth, foster organizational improvement, and strengthen a powerful collective voice. At their worst, they waste valuable resources and inhibit the success levels of their members.

If your board belongs to a professional organization, is contemplating membership, or is considering membership renewal, this chapter will help you evaluate the actual or potential value of that membership.

Is Membership for You?
"What's in it for me?" is the first and most appropriate question to ask when considering membership. How will membership enhance your ability to govern? What

positive impact has membership had, or will it likely have, on you, your fellow board members, and your organization?

Although membership services vary greatly, all professional associations should provide the following core services.

A BIG WELCOME

Your decision to join or to renew membership is a big deal. For you, it represents a significant investment of time and money. For the association, it provides the opportunity to deliver services that meet or exceed your expectations.

Keep in mind that top-flight associations don't take your membership for granted. To them the words "in service to you" amount to more than a motto; they're a way of doing business.

BOARD MEMBER EDUCATION

Professional development is at the heart of membership services. As a member, you should expect outstanding opportunities to engage with and learn from experts through conferences, quarterly or monthly publications, short courses, seminars, and online offerings. Some associations have formalized their educational programs by themselves, offering or partnering with universities to deliver educational services that lead to academic credit or professional certification.

NETWORKING AND BOARD MEMBER DEVELOPMENT

Networking provides important opportunities to capitalize on the talents and experiences of others and to develop your skills through participation on committees and task forces that address issues of consequence to your organization. Expect to meet and interact with other association members, government and private-sector leaders, industry experts, service providers, and vendors in both formal and informal settings.

ADVOCACY

Every professional association touts its ability to advocate for its members' wants and needs. Many employ long-standing processes to develop and advance organizational interests and to influence the development of public policy in ways that meet their wants and needs. However, it's a good idea to look beyond process and instead examine the results of its advocacies. Are the association's advocacy efforts making significant differences in terms of decisions that are favorable to the association and its members?

Obtaining answers to the following questions will help you evaluate the results of organizational advocacy.

1. Is the association advocating for all members' interests equally? Is advocacy aimed at the

needs of big players or coalitions, or does it represent all members?

2. Exactly what have recent advocacy efforts accomplished? Remember: advocacy is not just about fighting the good fight; it's about results that meet the wants and needs of the association's members.

3. Determine whether the association initiates change or whether it responds to changes proposed by others. Basically, does it lead or follow? Knowing that will give you insight into whether it is primarily proactive or reactive.

4. Does the association have the capability and capacity to develop or alter advocacy positions on short notice? What mechanisms are in place to rapidly respond to changes in the environment, and what evidence shows they work?

TECHNICAL ASSISTANCE

Professional associations exist in part to provide services that members need but cannot or do not provide for themselves. They should offer such services as policy guidance/development, planning, dispute resolution, executive searches, political strategy, bargaining services and/or support, data collection and management, constituent outreach strategies, professional standards, and evaluation tools.

Although members can access technical assistance from private-sector providers, professional associations often broker services through preferred provider arrangements or have a list of recommended providers for their members.

PROFESSIONAL STANDARDS

The association should be the source of professional standards for its members. As such, it should provide ethics training for new and continuing members and should model its own ethical standards at all times.

INFORMATION SOURCE

Expect the association to keep you well-informed about local, state, and national issues and events that are likely to affect you. An important part of keeping you in the know is to point out media and interest-group spin on issues. In effect, the association is your listening ear that monitors events and issues on your behalf so you don't have to do so.

INFLUENCE

An association is a force to be reckoned with when it provides an ever-present reasoned voice, accurately represents the collective interests of its members, and successfully communicates those interests. To check out an association's influence, ask around.

Association Power

Association power results from clarity of purpose, strength of commitment, skill at deployment, and the ability to constantly improve. The following are good indicators of an association's power.

- **First Is Clarity.** Clarity is accomplished when ideas about what matters most are subjected to intense judgment and scrutinized from every angle. Only those associations that are willing to explore and resolve potentially divisive issues can achieve the type of clarity that equates to rock-solid positions for which all members are willing to fight.

- **Second Is Commitment.** Commitment is the line in the sand from which the association will not retreat. Driven by principle, obligation, or relationship, commitment is what generates the power and momentum necessary to excel.

- **Third Is Deployment.** Deployment is action beyond talk. It's making sure the right people get the right information delivered the right way at the right time and are prepared to put it to use.

- **Fourth Is Improvement.** Associations that evaluate their results with an eye toward improving their services and processes perform at a higher level over time and acquire power that translates to positive results.

ANNUAL CONFERENCE

As the organization's capstone event, the annual conference by itself should be worth the price of your membership. If it's not, you're being shortchanged.

Typically, the annual conference is the association's largest, lengthiest, and most comprehensive gathering. Expect it to include expert presentations, break-out sessions, policy workshops, a business meeting, lunches, a banquet, networking opportunities, and access to service providers and vendors.

QUESTIONING PROFESSIONAL ASSOCIATIONS

1. If your board belongs to a professional association, does it actively participate in the association's events and utilize its services?
2. Are you satisfied that the professional association understands issues faced by your board and advocates effectively on your behalf?
3. Does the association's governing board reflect the makeup of its membership in terms of large or small organizational members, urban or rural settings, cultural backgrounds, geographic areas, and other criteria that apply to member organizations?

4. Does the association have a strategic plan to guide its activities, and if so, does it follow the plan, track its progress, and report its performance to members?

5. Which service provided by the association do you consider most important? Which service do you consider least important to your board?

ONE FINAL POINT

High-performing associations know they cannot be all things to all people. It's their habit to take deliberate and often difficult steps to forge agendas that recognize and respond to their members' most pressing needs. In doing so, they overcome barriers to success that stop other organizations.

Chapter 9
Board Self-Evaluation

A Matter of Perspective

Gaining a commitment from some governing boards to evaluate their own performance is a tough sell. They reject that level of accountability, saying they are evaluated by voters or those who appointed them. Others who are reluctant to evaluate their own performance are quick to point out that even though they have ultimate authority over the organization, they feel as if they have one arm tied behind their back when it comes to controlling results. The way they see it: their board sets the course but doesn't steer the ship; it creates policies and approves plans but doesn't implement them; the budget is mostly an ongoing commitment with little wiggle room for their priorities; they are the final authority but delegate direct control of the organization to the CEO; and most issues that come before them are either before-the-fact proposals or after-the-fact reports. Given their beliefs and actions, is it any wonder they are reluctant to measure their own performance?

On the flip side are governing boards with totally different perspectives regarding the importance of evaluating their performance. They know that although boards do not directly control their organizations' day-to-day activities, they do decide their organizations' purpose and structure and have final authority over all resources, plans, goals, and accountability measures. Such boards are results focused and work closely with their CEOs to monitor organizational progress.

Boards that take self-evaluation seriously understand that they provide the only continuous leadership for their organization. Individual leaders may come and go, but the board is ever present. Because of that, the board's performance is the most decisive factor in the success of the organization. Boards that hold themselves to high standards of performance demonstrate leadership and accountability by example.

A CLOSER LOOK AT BOARD SELF-EVALUATION
MEASUREMENT CRITERIA

If your board does not currently evaluate its performance or if you're not sure it's doing a good job of evaluating its performance, where can you turn to learn what should be included in an evaluation?

Professional associations are among the best sources of information. As part of your membership fee, expect them to provide you with: (1) information about objective performance standards, (2) evaluation formats, (3) current research, (4) best-practices information, and (5) training regarding board self-evaluation.

If your board does not belong to a professional association, you can access the information you need either online or through private-sector consultants.

WHAT TO MEASURE

There is general agreement that board self-evaluation should address both individual board member performance and performance of the board as a whole. Individual formats for measuring board performance vary greatly; however, they generally include measuring the following areas of board performance.

- Use of guiding ideas to monitor and measure organizational performance
- Use of board processes to conduct meetings
- Board-CEO relationship
- Performance relative to financial oversight
- Performance relative to oversight of capital assets
- Individual performance relative to board standards and ethics
- Advocacy on behalf of the organization

QUESTIONING BOARD SELF-EVALUATION

1. Does your board conduct a formal self-evaluation annually?

2. Is your board satisfied with the current evaluation process?

3. Are individual board member evaluations anonymous, or are names attached to the comments and ratings?

4. What areas of board performance were identified as growth areas during the most recent evaluation, and what progress has the board made regarding them?

5. How does your board know that the self-evaluation process reflects current best practices?

ONE FINAL POINT

If accountability for performance doesn't start with the board, it is a weakened device for the entire organization. Actions speak louder than words.

Chapter 10
Board Politics

You may not consider yourself a politician, but you are. There's no way to get around it: board governance is political. It's political because it requires decision making about where to direct limited resources and involves the exercise of power, authority, and influence. With those decisions comes the heat, so be ready.

Arbiter and Protector of Stakeholder Interests

As mentioned in chapter 6, the board is the arbiter and protector of stakeholder interests. That means your board is responsible for attending to the needs, rights, limits, priorities, wants, and expectations of individuals and groups that have interests in your organization.

For boards, the challenges are significant, as illustrated by the following three examples.

- A municipal assembly decides to use some of its tax revenue to boost the town's economy by supporting local nonprofits. The assembly solicits proposals for funding and finds that requests significantly exceed the amount of funding available. How does the assembly fairly and equitably allocate the funding?

- A statewide professional association's membership is composed of organizations representing both large urban communities and small rural ones. There's a constant tension between the rural members and the urban members in terms of the association's governing-board seat allocation, organizational priorities, and demands for resource prioritization. How does the organization balance diverse wants and expectations and satisfy its membership?

- A local school board struggles with flat funding and rising costs but still wants to invest more in technology for its classrooms. In response to the board's priority, the school administration has proposed budget cuts to certain sports and fine-arts programs as a way of increasing the commitment to technology. Now what?

    You get the idea: board decisions involve politics.

Charting Your Course

Some board members begin their service by holding themselves to high personal and professional standards but, over time, discover it's easier to trim their sails with the political winds rather than sail against them, even if that means sacrificing their standards. The downside, of course, is that eventually, they're likely to end up somewhere they don't want to be—supporting something they're unable to explain to those they represent.

Successfully navigating the ever-shifting waters of governance is not easy; times change, advantage shifts, and opportunities arise that challenge principles. When you're a new board member, your best course is to check your ethics compass frequently, because there will be numerous invitations to stray from the course you've set for yourself. This is another area where having a mentor is of great value; mentors can often see traps and pitfalls that are invisible to new board members.

IN SERVICE TO OTHERS

Board members bring diverse points of view to the table, and a board's ability to manage those points of view both individually and collectively speaks to its skill, discipline, and character. When reason and respect prevail, a diversity of views becomes a strength for crafting decisions that improve board relationships and maximize stakeholder benefits. If competing ideologies and disregard take precedence over civility and respect, organizational results are diminished and stakeholder interests are not well served.

Your stakeholders—whether voters, healthcare consumers, schoolchildren, community members, retirees, or members of a religious group or condo association—are counting on you to represent them. They expect nothing less than your best behavior, keenest judgment, and most assiduous efforts, as well as the most favorable results you can produce. In their view, you and your fellow board members are in service to them.

QUESTIONING BOARD POLITICS

1. In your board's most recent self-evaluation, how did it rate itself on ethical behavior?
2. Do your organization's bylaws address board member ethics?
3. Has your board received professional development training in dealing with the politics of governance?
4. On a scale of 1 to 5, with 5 being the highest, how would you rate your board's ability to successfully manage the politics of governance?
5. What do you consider to be the board's greatest political challenge?

ONE FINAL POINT

As you begin your board service, keep in mind that when big-time issues come before the board, it's best to stake out your position as early as possible. Pressure mounts on fence-sitters, and they're often used unethically by those who seek political gain.

CHAPTER 11
HIGH-PERFORMING BOARDS

Have you ever noticed how organizations that exist for identical purposes operating in similar circumstances with comparable resources and opportunities can produce results that are dramatically different? As a general rule, a few excel, most perform at acceptable levels, and some struggle just to stay in operation.

While the causes for their variations in performance may be complex and difficult to understand from an outsider's viewpoint, their observable governance practices are not.

The ten previous chapters have addressed the basics of sound governance. This chapter identifies a few additional practices that are typical of boards that govern high-performing organizations.

LONG-TERM FOCUS

Boards that govern high-performing organizations know where they're going and have long-term plans to get there. These boards actively monitor organizational progress and demand fact-based performance updates on a regular basis. They know their organizations' capabilities and capacities and take steps to ensure that plans and performance targets challenge but do not overwhelm.

Driven by their mission, vision, values, goals, and objectives, these boards are frugal with their resources and stringent regarding their expectations. As one CEO put it, "If something is not in our long-term plan and the board didn't budget for it, it's basically not going to happen." That type of discipline insulates the board from pressure to place others' wants ahead of the organization's mission.

These boards don't take performance for granted. Their governance approach is to trust but verify. They know that what gets measured gets done, so they predetermine performance expectations and set up fact-based systems to track organizational performance.

Boards of successful organizations follow a basic rule: plan the work, work the plan, measure what matters.

Use of Committees

While the use of committees is a common board practice, high-performing boards are definite about the purpose, structure, and use of committees. It's their practice to:

- Assign important and appropriate tasks.
- Clearly define committee roles, responsibilities, and authority.

- Ensure strong support and guidance.
- Include the right people on committees.
- Appropriately recognize committees for their work.

PROFESSIONAL SERVICES PROVIDERS

Professional services providers are typically attorneys, architects, accountants, and other consultants that provide specific services the organization uses occasionally and/or does not have staff to perform.

Wise use of professional services allows boards to plan and predict with greater accuracy, head off potential problems, position themselves to take advantage of opportunities, and perform at higher levels. As is the case with committees, high-performing boards are very deliberate in their expectations of and relationships with professional services providers. Following are steps boards can take to maximize their professional-services-provider relationships.

- Communicate board goals, plans, priorities, and expectations to service providers at the beginning of your relationship, and update them annually.
- Use professional advice primarily to shape decisions and prevent problems. Sound advice consistently applied is less expensive than occasional advice intensely applied.
- Address concerns with professional services providers as they arise; unattended issues magnify and distort relationships.

- Seek the input of professional services providers when conducting board self-evaluations, because their input can raise levels of board success.
- Professional services providers offer their best judgments; however, final responsibility for decisions rests with the board.

OPERATING ENVIRONMENT

The following illustration depicts the factors that influence a governing board's operating environment. Board policy, shown within the confines of the rectangle, is solely the prerogative of the board. High-performing boards maximize their policy opportunity by creating and applying policies that make full use of their power and authority.

The outside of the rectangle identifies legal constraints that limit a board's power and authority. Savvy boards have learned to capitalize on their imposed limitations and use them as both a sword and a shield. As a shield, the external limitations protect the board's authority to govern within specific limits. As a sword, the external requirements grant and clarify significant authority for the board to exercise its power and control over the organization and to operate as a legal entity.

Table 4

Negotiated Agreements

Laws — **Board Policy** — Regulations

Court Decisions

QUESTIONING HIGH-PERFORMING BOARDS

1. What systems does your board have in place to track and monitor organizational performance?
2. How does your board balance short-term needs with long-term goals?
3. If your board employs a committee structure, does it evaluate the performance of that structure as part of its annual self-evaluation?
4. Does your board evaluate the performance of its professional services providers and review that data with them?
5. If you could make one change that would improve the performance of your board, what would it be?

THE FINAL POINT

High-performing boards have mastered the basics and developed skill in the nuances of governance. They appreciate that politics is part of their landscape and have learned to succeed in an often politically charged environment. While these boards are unique in many ways, the factor common to them all is their discipline and intense desire to make things better for their chosen cause.